TABLE OF CONTENTS

INTRODUCTION

Have you ever found yourself pondering, "Why aren't readers discovering my books, and why aren't sales flowing in?" It's that authentic, human moment of uncertainty, standing there, scratching your head, contemplating what might be holding your creations back. There's this innate yearning for recognition, a deep desire to see your literary creations embraced by readers. The bewilderment sets in, prompting questions like, "What's the missing link? Why isn't the hard work translating into the success I envisioned?" It's a relatable struggle, a genuine quest for answers in the expansive realm of publishing, where every author grapples with the same query: What's the secret sauce to make my books stand out? Well, this book will be your solution to all your unanswered queries.

Well, fear not. This book is more than a reflection on those unanswered questions; it's the guide you've been searching for. Within these pages, you'll discover the solutions, the strategies, and the secret sauce to propel your books into the limelight and captivate the readers you've been yearning for.

DEDICATION

This book is a heartfelt dedication to all those starting their journey in self-publishing. As you delve into its pages, you'll uncover the deep secrets of the publishing world—from crafting exciting book covers to discovering the seven backend keywords, ensuring your book finds its perfect niche, and ultimately bringing your creation into the hands of readers. Throughout this journey, the book aims to provide you with valuable insights into every facet of publishing, making your foray into the world of literature a guided and fulfilling experience. Welcome to the exciting journey of self-publishing, where every page is a step toward realizing your literary aspirations.

CHAPTER 1

UNDERSTANDING SELF-PUBLISHING

Self-publishing is a way for authors to independently bring their work to the public without traditional publishing houses. Authors take on roles like editing, designing, and marketing their books. It offers creative freedom but also requires effort in navigating the publishing process and promoting the work to reach a wider audience. Self-publishing success often relies on a combination of writing skills, dedication, and effective self-promotion strategies.

What Self-Publishing is All About

So, what's the buzz about self-publishing? It's not just a method; it's a journey where you, the author, lead. Picture this: you're not just crafting stories; you're navigating the entire publishing ship. From when to set sail to the final destination, it's all in your hands.

Self-publishing is about freedom. The freedom to express your creativity without the constraints of traditional publishing. You decide when your book sees the light, what it looks like, and how it reaches readers. It's your story, your way.

Sure, there are challenges—every adventure has them. But those challenges add spice to the journey. Think of them as plot twists in your literary narrative, making the whole process all the more exciting.

Why Niche, Keywords, and Titles Matter

Now, let's talk about the power trio: Niche, Keywords, and Titles. Your niche is like your writing sanctuary. It's not just about picking a category; it's about finding your comfortable space, a place where your voice resonates and readers find solace.

Keywords, those silent guides in the digital realm, boost your book's discoverability. Embrace them as your best friends. We'll explore why they matter and how to use them effectively. It's like giving your book a map to navigate the vast online landscape.

Titles are your book's first impression. Crafting titles isn't just about naming; it's an art. We'll talk about creating titles that not only stand out but also beckon readers to explore. Think of it as creating a magnetic pull that's hard to resist.

CHAPTER 2

MASTERING NICHE SELECTION

Welcome to the second chapter of your self-publishing escapade—Mastering Niche Selection. Here, let's dive into finding that perfect niche for your literary playground. Let's break it down:

How to Pick the Perfect Niche

Selecting a niche isn't just about throwing darts at a genre board. It's a thoughtful process. Imagine it like choosing your favorite dish from a vast menu. We'll explore practical steps, consider your interests, and ensure you're not just picking a niche; you're finding a cozy corner in the literary world where your voice feels at home.

Start by taking a moment for some introspection. What are your passions? What topics genuinely excite you? Identify your interests, hobbies, and the subjects you could talk about for hours. This is the foundation of your niche.

Get your detective hat on and dive into market research. Explore bestseller lists, popular genres, and upcoming trends in the literary world. Identify what's currently in demand and where there might be gaps waiting to be filled.

Figuring Out What Readers Want

Who are you writing for? Define your target audience. Consider demographics, interests, and preferences. Understanding your potential readership will guide your niche selection to align with their desires.

Look at what other authors in your potential niche are doing. Analyze their books, reader reviews, and overall engagement. Identify what works well and areas where you could bring a fresh perspective.

Assess your expertise and knowledge. What do you bring to the table that sets you apart? Consider your unique experiences, skills, or insights that can shape your niche and make your voice distinctive.

Finding Your Passionate Niche

Cross-reference your identified niche with your passions. Does it align with what genuinely excites you? Your niche should be a blend of market demand and personal enthusiasm to keep your writing fueled with authentic passion.

CHAPTER 3

CRAFTING TITLES THAT GRAB ATTENTION

Welcome to the chapter on Crafting Titles That Grab Attention, where we're about to unravel the secrets of turning your book title into a magnetic force.

Crafting Titles That Stand Out

Creating a title isn't just a formality; it's a chance to make a lasting impression. Think of your title as the face of your book, the first thing readers encounter. Crafting titles that stand out involves injecting a unique flair.

Start by understanding the essence of your book. What emotions does it evoke? Is there a central theme or feeling you want to convey? Craft your title to include an element of surprise or the unexpected.

Readers are drawn to the unknown, so weaving an intriguing twist into your title can create that irresistible urge to uncover more.

Create a subtle sense of urgency in your title. Whether it's a question that demands an answer or a hint at a limited opportunity, instilling a bit of time sensitivity can prompt readers to click for more details.

Before finalizing your title, test it with a small audience or beta readers. Get their reactions and gauge if the title stirs the intended emotions. Their feedback can be invaluable in refining and perfecting your title.

Take feedback seriously. If beta readers or your target audience suggest tweaks, be open to fine-tuning your title. Sometimes, small adjustments can make a significant impact.

If your book has cultural or niche elements, ensure your title resonates within that context. A title that aligns with cultural nuances can be more compelling to the target audience.

What Makes a Title Irresistible

Pinpoint the emotions you want your readers to feel. Whether it's excitement, nostalgia, or curiosity, identify the core emotions your book encapsulates. This emotional connection forms the backbone of an irresistible title. Brainstorm words that evoke the emotions you've identified. Think beyond the obvious and explore a range of descriptive terms. This list will serve as your palette for crafting a title that packs an emotional punch.

Alliteration isn't just a tongue-twisting literary device; it's a tool to make your title memorable. Experiment with repeating sounds or consonants that enhance the rhythm of your title. It adds a musical quality that lingers in the reader's mind.

While crafting an irresistible title, ensure it remains clear and easy to understand. Avoid overly complex or convoluted phrases. A title should pique interest without confusion.

Examples and Formulas for Killer Titles

Let's get practical. Crafting a killer title is like cooking, and every chef needs their recipes. We'll dive into real examples, breaking down what worked wonders for other authors. From the rhythm of words to the power of alliteration, we'll explore formulas that turn your title from ordinary to extraordinary.

Consider how your title resonates emotionally. Does it evoke curiosity, joy, or suspense? Emotion is the secret ingredient that connects readers to your book on a deeper level.

Crafting killer titles involves a mix of creativity, emotion, and a dash of intrigue. Here are examples across different genres to illustrate the diversity of effective titles:

1. **Mystery/Thriller:**
   - "Whispers in the Shadows"
   - "The Silent Conspiracy"
   - "Echoes of Deceit"

2. **Romance:**
   - "Love Beyond the Pages"
   - "Whirlwind Hearts"
   - "Sunset Serenade"

3. **Science Fiction:**
   - "Quantum Echoes"
   - "Stellar Nexus"
   - "Chronicles of Cyberspace"

4. **Self-Help/Motivational:**
   - "Ignite Your Spark: A Guide to Unleashing Potential"
   - "Fearless Living: Embrace the Journey"
   - "Bold Choices, Bright Tomorrow"

5. **Historical Fiction:**
   - "Echoes of Eternity: A Tudor Tale"
   - "Ripples in Time: A Civil War Chronicle"
   - "The Silk Road Odyssey"

6. **Fantasy:**
   - "Sorcery's Embrace: Chronicles of Eldoria"
   - "Enchanting Shadows: Quest for the Lost Realm"
   - "Wings of Celestial Magic"

7. **Memoir:**
   - "Bridges of Resilience: My Journey Beyond Adversity"
   - "Uncharted Horizons: A Life Unveiled"
   - "Footprints in the Sand: A Memoir of Endurance"

8. **Business/Entrepreneurship:**
   - "Strategic Visionaries: Navigating the Business Frontier"
   - "The Innovation Blueprint: Building Tomorrow's Success"
   - "Profitable Paradigms: Entrepreneurial Wisdom Unveiled"

Remember, these examples aim to capture the essence of different genres and styles. The key is to tailor your title to fit your specific book, audience, and the emotions you aim to evoke.

CHAPTER 4

CRACKING THE KEYWORD CODE

Begin by distilling the essence of your book into key themes and topics. What are the core elements that define your work? These form the foundation for the keywords that will enhance discoverability.

Identify successful books in your genre. Analyze their titles, descriptions, and the keywords they employ. This helps you understand the language your target readers use and discover effective keywords.

Create a seed list of potential keywords. These are the fundamental terms directly related to your book. Include genres, themes, and unique aspects. This list serves as the starting point for your keyword research.

Why Keywords Are Your Best Friends

In the crowded space of online bookstores, keywords act as the spotlight for your work. Choosing the right keywords related to your book's genre, themes, and target audience enhances its discoverability. This practical approach ensures that your masterpiece doesn't get lost in the vast sea of books available online. It's like having a book blurb that not only entices readers but also ensures your book surfaces in relevant searches.

Keywords help you reach your intended audience. If your self-published book falls into a specific niche or caters to a particular demographic, incorporating relevant keywords ensures that it reaches the right readers.

Incorporate long-tail keywords—specific, multi-word phrases that cater to niche searches. They often have less competition and can attract a more targeted audience. Analyze reviews of similar books in your genre. Readers often use language that mirrors potential search queries. Extract keywords from these reviews to enhance your list. Keep an eye on the performance of your chosen keywords over time. Don't forget to include relevant keywords in your book's back matter. This ensures that even readers who have finished your book can contribute to its discoverability.

Remember, the key is not just to select keywords but to continually refine and adapt based on real-time data and reader engagement.

Tools to Help You Nail the Right Keywords

Explore specialized keyword research tools like Google Keyword Planner, Helium, Jungle Scout, AMZ Suggestion Expander, Google Trends, Self-Publishing Titans Keyword

Research and Niche Tools, Asinseed, Chatgpt4, Publisher Rocket, or SEMrush. These tools provide insights into the search volume and competition for specific keywords. Identify high-ranking and relevant terms.

Keep an eye on the performance of your chosen keywords over time. Tools like Amazon Author Central or Google Analytics can provide valuable insights. Adjust your keyword strategy based on changing trends and audience behavior.

Writing Descriptions That Get Noticed

Understanding your potential readers is the first step in creating a book description that captivates. Begin with an attention-grabbing introduction, setting the tone for your unique story. Convey the core themes, providing readers with a glimpse into the heart of your narrative.

Invoke emotions that resonate with your book's tone, making your description more than a summary but an immersive experience. Use descriptive language to create vivid imagery, allowing readers to visualize your world and connect with the emotions of your characters.

Compellingly introduce your characters, highlighting their uniqueness and the challenges they face. Keep the description concise yet impactful, leaving readers intrigued and eager to uncover the full story. When potential readers come across your book, they often read the description to decide if it's what they're looking for. Strategic use of keywords in your book description can make it more compelling and search engine-friendly. Craft your book description to spark curiosity and create a lasting impression.

CHAPTER 5

BUILDING YOUR AUTHOR PRESENCE

Building a Brand That Readers Love

Start by defining your author's brand. What themes, genres, or values represent you as a writer? This is the foundation of your author's presence.

Establish a central hub for your online presence—a user-friendly author website. Include a bio, book details, and a blog to engage with your audience.

Select social media platforms aligned with your audience. Engage regularly, share insights into your writing process, and connect authentically with readers and fellow authors.

Navigating Social Media and Blogs

Join writing communities, both online and offline. Contribute, seek advice, and build relationships with fellow authors. This not only expands your network but also provides valuable insights.

Optimize your author profiles on platforms like Amazon, Goodreads, and social media. Use compelling author bios, high-quality photos, and consistent branding.

Regularly create content that resonates with your brand. This could be blog posts, social media updates, or even short stories. Consistency is key.

Connecting Authentically with Your Audience

Actively engage with your readers. Respond to comments, host Q&A sessions, and show appreciation for their support. Building a loyal readership is a cornerstone of a strong author presence.

Collaborate with fellow authors on joint projects, interviews, or promotions. This cross-promotion introduces you to new audiences and strengthens your author network. Attend book signings, literary festivals, and writing conferences. These events not only provide exposure but also offer opportunities to connect with readers and industry professionals.

Launch a newsletter to directly connect with your audience. Share exclusive content, updates, and behind-the-scenes glimpses. This creates a more personal connection with your readers.

Remember, building your author's presence is a journey, not a sprint. Stay authentic, be patient, and enjoy the process of connecting with your readers and fellow authors. Your presence is not just about selling books; it's about building a community around your passion for storytelling.

CHAPTER 6

WRITING AND EDITING LIKE A PRO

Tips for Writing Efficiently

Begin by setting clear writing goals. Define what you want to achieve with your writing—whether it's completing a certain word count, finishing a chapter, or achieving a specific writing milestone.

Create a consistent writing routine. Dedicate specific times for writing, minimizing distractions. Consistency fosters productivity and helps you build a writing habit.

When writing your first draft, focus on getting your ideas on paper without overthinking perfection. Embrace imperfections, knowing that the editing stage is where you refine and polish your work.

After finishing a writing session, engage in self-editing. Review and refine what you've written, addressing obvious errors and refining the flow. This initial self-editing stage streamlines the later editing process.

The Importance of Professional Editing

So, you've poured your heart and soul into your manuscript. It's your baby, your creation, and you're probably thinking it's good to go, right? Well, here's the thing – the magic happens when you bring in a professional editor.

Imagine you've been staring at the same painting for days. You might miss that one tiny stroke that's slightly off. The same goes for your writing. A professional editor brings a fresh set of eyes, catching those nuances you might have overlooked. Your writing is like a diamond in the rough. A professional editor knows how to cut and polish, making it shine. They refine your sentences, iron out awkward phrasing, and ensure your message comes across crystal clear.

Let's face it – grammar can be a sneaky little troublemaker. Professional editors are the grammar guardians you need. They spot those pesky typos, correct grammar slip-ups, and ensure your writing is as polished as it gets.

Ever worry that your characters might be doing a time-traveling dance with their ages? Or that your tone does a flip from casual to formal without warning? A professional editor keeps your writing consistent, maintaining that smooth reading experience.

Editors know what makes readers tick. They put themselves in the reader's shoes, asking the vital question – does this make sense? Is it engaging? They ensure your work isn't just a masterpiece to you but to the wider audience.

Writing is like music, and an editor is your conductor. They ensure your words flow seamlessly, creating a rhythm that captivates readers. No awkward pauses or out-of-tune sentences – just a symphony of words.

Let's be real – putting your work out there can be nerve-wracking. Having a professional editor gives you that boost of confidence. Your manuscript isn't just good; it's polished, refined, and ready to make an impact.

Getting Honest Feedback from Beta Readers

Once you've completed a significant portion of your manuscript, share it with beta readers. Their fresh perspective can provide valuable insights into areas that may need improvement or clarification.

Leverage writing tools like Grammarly, ProWritingAid, or Hemingway Editor to catch grammar, style, and readability issues. These tools complement your editing efforts and enhance the overall quality of your writing.

Read your work aloud to identify awkward phrasing, pacing issues, or repetitive patterns. Hearing your words helps you catch nuances that may go unnoticed when reading silently. Strive for clarity and conciseness in your writing. Ensure your ideas are communicated effectively, avoiding unnecessary complexity. Use straightforward language to convey your message.

When editing, take breaks between sessions. This helps you approach your work with fresh eyes, making it easier to spot errors or areas that need improvement.

Join writing groups or find an accountability partner. Sharing your progress and challenges with others creates a supportive environment that motivates you to stay on track.

Remember, the writing and editing process is iterative. Embrace the journey, stay open to feedback, and celebrate the progress you make along the way. Writing like a pro is not about perfection but about the continuous improvement of your craft.

CHAPTER 7

DESIGNING COVERS THAT SPEAK VOLUMES

Elements of a Cover That Sells

Get cozy with your genre. Different genres have different vibes, and your cover should vibe with your readers. Research the top covers in your genre for inspiration.

Less is often more. Aim for simplicity. A cluttered cover can confuse potential readers. Focus on a central theme or image that encapsulates your book.

Choose fonts wisely. Your title should be legible even in thumbnail size. Experiment with font styles that match your book's tone, and ensure readability.

Colors evoke emotions. Think about the mood of your book. Vibrant, muted, bold – choose a color palette that aligns with your story's vibe.

They say a picture is worth a thousand words. Your cover image should tell a story. Whether it's a symbolic object, a character, or a scene, make it resonate with your book's essence.

Your cover will be seen in thumbnail size online. Test its

effectiveness by shrinking it down. If it's still striking and clear, you're on the right track. Ensure your title and any text stand out against the background. Contrast helps your words pop, making them easily readable.

If you're writing a series, maintain a consistent design theme. This builds brand recognition, and readers love a cohesive series on their bookshelf.

Share your cover options with friends, fellow writers, or your target audience. Honest feedback helps you refine your design and ensures it resonates with potential readers.

Hiring a Great Designer

If design isn't your forte, consider hiring a professional. A skilled designer can turn your vision into a polished, market-ready cover.

Testing Your Cover for Maximum Impact

Remember, your cover is the first impression your book makes. It's like a handshake with your reader. Make it firm, memorable, and reflective of the amazing story within.

CHAPTER 8

SETTING THE RIGHT PRICE

Finding the Sweet Spot for Your Book

Get the lowdown on what similar books in your genre are priced at. Are you in the realm of bestsellers, mid-range, or budget-friendly reads? Understanding your market is step one.

Take a peek at what it costs you to produce your book. This includes editing, cover design, and any other expenses. Factor in your time – it's valuable too. What's your aim with this book?

Using Promotions and Discounts Effectively

Plan discounts and promotions strategically. Whether it's a limited-time offer or a special occasion promo, these can spike interest and boost sales. Be competitive. While you want your book to stand out, pricing way above the norm might turn potential readers away.

Balancing Profit and Market Appeal

Clarify your aim with this book. Are you aiming for widespread readership, or is exclusivity more your style? Your pricing strategy aligns with your goals.

If you're offering both eBook and print versions, consider pricing them differently. Print books generally cost more due to production and distribution. For new releases or series starters, consider an introductory price to entice early readers. It's like a welcome gift for those who jump on board from the get-go.

Find the sweet spot that reflects your book's value. Don't be afraid to experiment. Test different price points and monitor how they affect sales. Adjust accordingly to find that perfect balance.

If you're going through a publishing platform, factor in their cut. Make sure your pricing still leaves you with a royalty that feels fair for your effort.

Put yourself in your reader's shoes. What would you be willing to pay for a book like yours? Be fair, be considerate, and think about the value you're providing.

Remember, setting the right price is a bit of an art. It's about finding that sweet spot where your book is not only worth every penny but also attractive to your ideal reader.

CHAPTER 9

CHOOSING PLATFORMS AND FORMATS

Exploring Different Publishing Platforms

Start by researching various publishing platforms like Amazon Kindle Direct Publishing (KDP), Draft2Digital IngramSpark, and others. Understand their fee structures, distribution networks, and user reviews.

Think about your publishing goals. Are you looking for maximum reach, ease of use, or specific distribution channels? Different platforms cater to different needs.

Consider the platform's user-friendliness. Choose one that aligns with your tech comfort level. A smoother process means less stress for you.

Look into royalty rates and costs associated with each platform. Some might have upfront fees, while others take a percentage of your sales. Ensure it fits your budget.

Check out the community and support offered by each platform. Forums, FAQs, and customer support can be lifesavers when navigating the publishing journey.

Deciding on eBook, Paperback, or Hardcover

Understand your target audience. Ebooks are convenient,

paperbacks are versatile, and hardcovers are often preferred for collector's editions. Tailor your formats to your readers.

Evaluate the production costs for each format. Ebooks are usually more cost-effective while printing and binding impact the cost of paperbacks and hardcovers.

Consider where your audience prefers to purchase books. Ebooks are dominant in online markets, while physical formats are essential for bookstores and events.

Think about your cover design concerning the format. Ebooks require a striking digital cover, while print covers need to consider spine width and back cover elements.

Be aware of formatting challenges. Ebooks may have different formatting requirements than print versions. Ensure your manuscript is prepared accordingly.

Remember, the choices you make here influence how your readers experience your work. So, whether you're diving into the world of digital or going old-school with a paperback, tailor your choices to meet your goals and your reader's preferences.

CHAPTER 10

PROMOTING YOUR BOOK WITH FLAIR

Strategies for Before Your Launch

Start teasing your book before the launch. Share sneak peeks, behind-the-scenes moments, or even a captivating quote. Create a countdown on social media to build anticipation.

Engage with your existing network. Whether it's friends, family, or fellow writers, get them excited about your upcoming release. Personal recommendations can go a long way.

Form a launch team of enthusiastic readers. Offer them early access or exclusive content in exchange for spreading the word. Their enthusiasm can create a ripple effect.

If possible, set up pre-orders. This not only generates early sales but can also boost your book's visibility on various platforms.

Reach out to influencers or bloggers in your genre. Offer them advanced copies for reviews or interviews. Their endorsement can significantly impact your book's reach.

Keeping the Buzz Going After Launch

Keep the momentum going on social media. Share reader reactions, snippets from reviews, and any noteworthy achievements. Encourage readers to share their experiences.

Consider running promotions post-launch, like discounted prices or bundled deals. This can reignite interest and attract new readers.

Host virtual or in-person author events. Readings, Q&A sessions, or even a virtual book club can keep the buzz alive and provide direct engagement with your audience.

Encourage readers to share their thoughts, photos, or even fan art related to your book. User-generated content adds authenticity to your promotion efforts.

Continue being active in writing communities. Share your journey, insights, or lessons learned. This ongoing engagement keeps you on the radar of potential readers.

Harnessing the Power of Reviews

Prioritize early review outreach. Send advanced copies to reviewers, both professionals and enthusiastic readers. Positive reviews build credibility and attract more readers.

Promptly encourage your readers to leave reviews after they've finished your book. Make it easy for them by providing links and expressing gratitude for their time.

Respond to reviews, both positive and constructive, with gratitude. Engage with your readers, and show appreciation for their insights. This interaction fosters a positive author-reader relationship.

Feature snippets from positive reviews in your marketing materials. Whether on your website, social media, or book promotions, these snippets act as endorsements that can sway potential readers.

Remember, book promotion is an ongoing journey. Keep the energy high, stay connected with your audience, and adapt your strategies based on the feedback and engagement you receive.

CHAPTER 11

OVERCOMING HURDLES

Conquering Writer's Block

When stuck, change your writing environment. A new setting can stimulate creativity. If you're indoors, step outside; if you're alone, try a bustling café.

Engage in freewriting exercises. Set a timer, and without worrying about structure or perfection, let your thoughts flow onto the page. This can help break through mental blocks.

Sometimes, stepping away is the best solution. Take short breaks, go for a walk, or indulge in a different creative activity. Fresh perspectives often emerge during downtime.

Try expressing your ideas through a different medium, like drawing or speaking into a voice recorder. Shifting the mode of expression can loosen the grip of writer's block.

Break your writing tasks into smaller, achievable goals. Completing these bite-sized tasks creates a sense of accomplishment, boosting your confidence to tackle larger challenges.

Dealing with Negative Reviews

Differentiate between constructive criticism and personal attacks. Embrace constructive feedback that offers insights into areas for improvement without taking it personally.

Shift your focus to positive reviews. Remember why you started writing and the readers who appreciate your work. Positive reinforcement can counterbalance the impact of negative reviews.

Use negative reviews as opportunities to learn and improve. Assess whether the criticisms hold merit and consider incorporating valuable feedback into your future writing.

Reach out to fellow writers or online communities for support. Share your experiences and seek advice. Connecting with others who've faced similar challenges can be reassuring.

Cultivate resilience. Understand that not every reader will connect with your work, and that's okay. Develop a mindset that allows you to bounce back from setbacks.

Adapting to Changes in the Publishing World

Regularly stay informed about industry changes. Follow publishing news, subscribe to newsletters, and participate in forums to understand shifts in trends and technologies.

Network with other authors, publishers, and industry professionals. Collaborative efforts and shared insights can help you adapt to changes more effectively.

Diversify your skills. Stay adaptable by acquiring additional skills related to writing, marketing, or technology. Being versatile enhances your ability to navigate changes.

Be open to experimenting with new publishing platforms or formats. Test the waters to see if emerging trends align with your writing style and audience.

If major changes are impacting your writing career, consider seeking professional guidance. Literary agents, publishing consultants, or writing organizations can offer valuable advice.

Remember, overcoming hurdles is an integral part of the writing journey. Embrace challenges as opportunities for growth, and don't hesitate to seek support when needed.

CHAPTER 12

EXPANDING YOUR REACH THROUGH AUDIOBOOKS

The Rise of Audiobooks: Understanding the Growing Market

- Begin by researching the current audiobook market. Identify trends, popular genres, and listener demographics. Platforms like Audible and market reports can provide valuable insights.

- Understand how your genre fits into the audiobook landscape. Some genres may have a higher demand for audiobooks, and aligning with these trends can enhance your reach.

- Study listener behavior. Know when and where your target audience listens to audiobooks. Tailor your release and marketing strategies based on peak listening times.

- Explore different audiobook platforms and their submission processes. Consider exclusive deals, royalty structures, and the platform's user interface when making your decision.

Audiobook Production: DIY vs. Professional Narration

- Honestly evaluate your narration skills. If you're confident in your ability to convey the story effectively, DIY may be an option. If not, consider professional narration.

- If going DIY, invest in quality recording equipment and soundproofing. Practice narration, focus on pacing, and ensure clear articulation. Edit the audio for a polished finish.

- If opting for professional narration, research and hire a reputable narrator. Provide them with detailed character descriptions and pronunciation guides to ensure an accurate performance.

- Regardless of the choice, prioritize audio quality. Remove background noise, ensure consistent volume, and listen critically to catch any potential issues.

Marketing Audiobooks: Tactics to Increase Visibility and Sales

- Tap into your existing reader base. Notify them about the audiobook release through newsletters, social

- media, and author websites. Encourage pre-orders for a strong launch.
- Consider promotional pricing or exclusive discounts for the audiobook launch. This can attract new listeners and incentivize your existing readers to explore the audio format.
- Collaborate with other authors or influencers in your genre for cross-promotion. Share snippets, and reviews, or even collaborate on joint audiobook launches to reach wider audiences.
- Leverage platforms like Instagram, TikTok, or YouTube to share engaging content related to your audiobook. Create teaser trailers, behind-the-scenes clips, or audiobook-specific Q&A sessions.
- Encourage listeners to leave reviews on audiobook platforms. Positive reviews build credibility and attract more listeners. Respond to reviews graciously and engage with your audience.

Remember, audiobooks offer a unique opportunity to connect with readers differently. Whether you choose the DIY route or opt for professional narration, thoughtful marketing strategies will amplify your audiobook's reach.

CHAPTER 13

LEVERAGING PODCASTS FOR AUTHOR BRANDING

Starting Your Author Podcast: From Concept to First Episode

- Identify a niche that aligns with your author's brand and interests your target audience. Whether it's discussing writing tips, book reviews, or industry insights, clarity on your podcast's focus is key.
- Determine the podcast format – solo commentary, interviews, panel discussions, or a combination. Tailor the format to your strengths and what resonates best with your audience.
- Plan your episodes. Create a content calendar outlining topics, guests, and release dates. Consistency is key to building a dedicated listener base.
- Acquire reliable recording equipment and editing tools. Clear audio quality is crucial for retaining listeners. Consider recording in a quiet environment or using noise-reduction software.

Guest Appearances: Reaching New Audiences through Podcast Interviews

- Research podcasts in your genre or niche. Identify those open to author interviews. Look for shows with an audience that aligns with your target readership.

- Develop a concise and engaging pitch for podcast hosts. Highlight your unique selling points, why you'd be an interesting guest, and what valuable insights or entertainment you can offer to their audience.

- Before the interview, familiarize yourself with the podcast's format and previous episodes. Prepare anecdotes, key messages, and book-related insights to share during the interview.

- Once the episode is live, actively promote it across your author platforms. Share on social media, newsletters, and your website. Encourage your audience to tune in and engage with the podcast host's community.

Podcast Promotion: Cross-Promotion and Social Media Strategies

- Collaborate with other podcasters in your niche for cross-promotion. Agree to promote each other's episodes to expand your reach and tap into new listener bases.

- Actively engage with your podcast audience on social media. Respond to comments, ask for feedback, and encourage listeners to share their thoughts and questions. This builds a community around your podcast.

- Create audiograms – short audio clips with visually appealing graphics – to share on social media. Audiograms are eye-catching and entice potential listeners to check out the full episode.

- Research relevant hashtags and trends in the podcasting community. Use them strategically in your social media posts to increase discoverability and engage with a broader audience.

- Reach out to influencers or authors with large followings. Invite them to share your podcast episode with their audience, expanding your reach and credibility.

Remember, the key to successful podcasting lies in consistent content creation, strategic promotion, and genuine engagement with your audience. As you navigate the podcasting realm, let your authentic voice shine and watch your author brand resonate with new audiences.

CHAPTER 14

NAVIGATING LITERARY EVENTS AND BOOK FAIRS

Preparing for Book Fairs: Booth Setup, Materials, and Networking

- Investigate the specific book fair you'll be attending. Understand the layout, target audience, and past exhibitors. Tailor your preparations to align with the fair's atmosphere.

- Design an inviting booth that reflects your author's brand. Consider the layout, visuals, and signage. Ensure your books are prominently displayed, and leave space for comfortable interaction with visitors.

- Prepare ample promotional materials. Bring copies of your books, business cards, bookmarks, and any merchandise. Create a visually appealing booth with banners or posters that showcase your book covers and author branding.

- Practice a friendly and approachable demeanor. Initiate conversations with attendees, share your passion for your work, and be ready to provide brief

- yet enticing summaries of your books.
- Have a method for collecting contact information from interested attendees. Use sign-up sheets or digital tools to build a mailing list for future updates and promotions.

Maximizing Literary Events: Panel Participation and Author Readings

- If participating in panels, thoroughly research the discussion topics. Familiarize yourself with fellow panelists and their work. Prepare talking points to contribute valuable insights during the discussion.
- If doing author readings, select engaging excerpts from your book. Practice reading aloud to ensure a smooth and captivating performance. Consider incorporating dramatic pauses and varied intonation to captivate your audience.
- Use panel participation and readings as opportunities to connect with event attendees. Attend networking sessions, answer questions, and participate in book signings to forge memorable interactions.
- Leverage social media and your author platform to inform your audience about your participation. Encourage followers to attend, and consider live-

tweeting or posting updates during the event.

Networking Strategies: Building Relationships with Industry Professionals

- Outline specific goals for networking, such as connecting with publishers, literary agents, or fellow authors. Research professionals, you want to meet and have a concise pitch ready about your work.
- Attend industry mixers, after-parties, or networking events associated with the literary event. These informal settings provide opportunities for relaxed conversations and relationship-building.
- Prepare professional business cards with your contact information, book covers, and author branding. Exchange cards with industry professionals and fellow authors you meet, adding a personal touch to each interaction.
- After the event, follow up with the contacts you made. Send personalized emails expressing gratitude for the connection and expressing interest in potential collaborations or partnerships.
- Maintain an active presence on social media platforms. Share highlights from the event, tag

- professionals you connected with, and continue engaging in conversations initiated during the event.

Navigating literary events and book fairs is not just about showcasing your work; it's an opportunity to build lasting connections in the literary community. Approach each interaction with authenticity and enthusiasm, and let your passion for storytelling shine through.

CHAPTER 15

UNDERSTANDING COPYRIGHT AND INTELLECTUAL PROPERTY

Navigating Copyright Laws: Protecting Your Creative Work

- Start by familiarizing yourself with copyright laws in your jurisdiction. Understand the basics, including what is automatically protected, the duration of protection, and the rights you hold as an author.

- Whenever you create original content, use the © symbol along with your name and the year of creation. This provides a visible indication of your copyright claim and can act as a deterrent against unauthorized use.

- While not mandatory, registering your work with the copyright office adds an extra layer of protection. It provides a public record of your ownership, making it easier to enforce your rights in case of infringement.

- Keep detailed records of when you create each piece of work. This can be crucial in establishing the

- timeline of your creation, especially in cases of potential disputes.

Licensing and Permissions: Properly Using Others Work in Your Writing

- Familiarize yourself with the concept of fair use, which allows limited use of copyrighted material without permission for purposes such as criticism, commentary, news reporting, teaching, scholarship, or research.

- If you plan to use someone else's copyrighted material beyond fair use, seek permission from the copyright holder. This often involves contacting the copyright owner directly and may include negotiating terms or paying licensing fees.

- Explore works in the public domain, as they are not protected by copyright. Public domain resources can be freely used without seeking permission.

- When using others' work under a license, adhere to the terms of that license. This may include providing attribution as specified by the license.

International Copyright Considerations: Expanding Your Global Reach

- Familiarize yourself with international copyright treaties, such as the Berne Convention. Understand the principles of these treaties, which often facilitate the recognition and protection of copyrights across borders.

- Recognize that copyright laws can vary significantly from one country to another. Before expanding your reach globally, research the copyright laws in specific countries where you intend to publish or distribute your work.

- In some cases, consider dual publication or simultaneous releases to ensure your work is protected across multiple jurisdictions. This can help you navigate different legal frameworks.

- If in doubt or dealing with complex international issues, seek legal advice from professionals specializing in intellectual property law. They can provide tailored guidance based on your specific situation.

Understanding copyright and intellectual property is crucial for safeguarding your creative work and respecting the rights of others. By following these practical steps, you can navigate the intricacies of copyright law in a way that protects your creations and fosters a respectful creative community.

CHAPTER 16

CRAFTING COMPELLING AUTHOR NEWSLETTERS

Building an Engaging Subscriber List: Strategies for Growth

- Develop enticing incentives, such as exclusive content, sneak peeks, or special promotions, to encourage visitors to subscribe. Ensure that your opt-in forms are strategically placed on your website and social media.

- Collaborate with other authors or relevant businesses for cross-promotions. This can expose your newsletter to new audiences who share similar interests.

- Host occasional giveaways, where entry involves subscribing to your newsletter. This not only attracts new subscribers but also engages your existing audience.

- Implement segmentation to tailor content based on subscriber preferences. This ensures that each subscriber receives content relevant to their interests,

- fostering a more personalized connection.

Content Creation: Balancing Promotions with Valuable Insights

- Set a regular newsletter schedule to manage reader expectations. Whether weekly, bi-weekly, or monthly, consistency is key for building reader trust and anticipation.

- Aim for a balance between promotional content (book releases, discounts) and value-driven content (author insights, writing tips). Provide content that resonates with your audience beyond just sales pitches.

- Share personal anecdotes, writing journeys, or behind-the-scenes glimpses. Connecting with readers on a personal level creates a sense of community and strengthens the author-reader relationship.

- Reward subscribers with exclusive content not available elsewhere. This could be early access to chapters, bonus scenes, or special author notes.

Analysing Newsletter Metrics: Adjusting Your Approach for Maximum Impact

- Monitor your newsletter's open and click-through rates. Identify trends in content that resonate with subscribers and adjust your future newsletters based on these insights.

- Evaluate subscriber engagement through metrics like interaction with calls-to-action, replies, and social shares. This helps gauge the effectiveness of your content in generating reader participation.

- Experiment with A/B testing for elements like subject lines, content format, or visuals. Analyse the results to understand what resonates best with your audience and refine your approach accordingly.

- Encourage subscribers to provide feedback through surveys or direct inquiries. Understanding their preferences and expectations enables you to tailor future newsletters to better meet their needs.

By implementing these practical steps, you'll not only build an engaged subscriber base but also create newsletters that provide value, foster connections, and adapt to the evolving preferences of your audience.

CHAPTER 17

TAPPING INTO FOREIGN MARKETS

Translating Your Work: Reaching Non-English-Speaking Audiences

- Identify target foreign markets by analysing book consumption patterns, cultural interests, and reading habits. Focus on regions where there is a demand for your genre or niche.

- Collaborate with experienced literary translators fluent in the target language. Ensure they understand the nuances of your work to convey its essence accurately. Seek recommendations or use reputable translation services.

- Begin with translations in languages with significant reader populations and potential for book sales. Consider languages spoken in multiple countries to maximize your reach.

- Whenever possible, plan simultaneous releases in your native language and the translated version. This creates anticipation and allows for coordinated marketing efforts.

Understanding Cultural Sensitivities: Adapting Your Message for Global Readers

- Familiarize yourself with cultural nuances, traditions, and sensitivities in the target market. Ensure your content respects local customs and does not inadvertently offend cultural norms.

- Employ sensitivity readers from the target culture to review your work. Their insights can highlight potential cultural misinterpretations and help you make informed adjustments.

- Customize your marketing materials to resonate with the cultural preferences of the target audience. This includes book covers, promotional imagery, and advertising content.

- Embrace diversity within your stories. Characters, settings, and themes that reflect a variety of cultures can enhance the universal appeal of your work.

Marketing Strategies for Foreign Markets: Localizing Your Approach

- Utilize popular local platforms for book distribution, sales, and promotions. Research region-specific online retailers and social media channels that cater to readers in the target market.

- Identify influential figures in the literary community or book blogging scene within the foreign market. Collaborate with them for book reviews, features, or promotions to tap into their established audience.
- Showcase your translated work at international book fairs to gain visibility and connect with potential readers. Leverage these events to network with local publishers, agents, and readers.
- Tailor promotional strategies to the economic and cultural context of the foreign market. Consider region-specific discounts, promotions, or exclusive content to entice readers.

By following these practical steps, you'll be better positioned to successfully tap into foreign markets, broaden your readership, and navigate the complexities of global literary engagement.

A WORD BY THE AUTHOR

Your opinion is valuable. If you enjoyed this book, I'd appreciate it if you could take a few moments to leave a heartfelt review. Your thoughtful feedback is greatly appreciated and vital. Thank you so much for taking the time to read this.

9 798224 734498